# Donna Payne's Pocket Guide to:

# Having Difficult Conversations about LGBT Discrimination

## Donna Payne

# CONTENTS

*Donna Payne's Pocket Guide To Having Difficult Conversations About LGBT Discrimination*

# ACKNOWLEDGMENTS

In Memory of my Grandmother, Emma Eliza Harris, who taught me to speak up for myself and become a force in the world.

**Book Editing by
Aisha Satterwhite of Straight Line Consultants**

**Cover Design by
Patricia Little of PNL Designs**

# INTRODUCTION

Throughout my time doing outreach in the Lesbian, Gay, Bisexual, and Transgender (LGBT) community, I have witnessed many difficult conversations. Every year, whether I am working with leaders who want to understand more or with students who are trying to handle family and school administrators, it always comes to this question – how do I have this difficult conversation? The basic thought of having the conversation makes people step away from the situation. It's not like I haven't had this fear. The first time I had a talk with a Minister about being a lesbian, my palms were sweaty, my voice became shaky and I had to go to the restroom every 5 minutes before the appointment. It was really bad because as a Black lesbian, talking to a Black Minister about the LGBT community was no joke! I was subject to maybe being thrown out of his office and told I was going to hell. I had begun preparing by using my own journey – the difficult conversation I'd had in the past with family and friends. But how was I to prepare effectively? There was no book to help me figure out this topic!

It doesn't have to be that way anymore. The good news is there are many ways to have a difficult conversation about supporting the LGBT community. You learn what works for you with experience. You can gain knowledge about how to have a healthy conversation right here. No lifetime experience of "what I should have or could have said" is needed. Just remember, this book is to help you sharpen your skills about what matters to you. In this great time of open dialogue about LGBT issues, there are so many difficult conversations quickly happening. The tools this book offers will be indispensable, very enlightening, and very useful. I am preparing you with the skills for a difficult conversation so you feel confident. I want you to feel as confident as I do when I talk to leaders of our religious and political world!


Let's begin.

Donna Payne

# CHAPTER 1
## Understanding Conflict around Lesbian, Gay, Bisexual, and Transgender (LGBT) Issues

When you are first preparing to have a difficult conversation, it is important to understand what is it about the subject that makes it hard. Sexuality has always been a sensitive and touchy subject. It gets even stickier when talking about sexual orientation or gender identity. Here are some of the main roadblocks that come up when you first begin discussing your support of LGBT issues:

- **Unresolved crisis – personal roadblocks based on home/work or religious background.**

In my work, I have learned that you never know a person's story until you open up and discuss your views. It is the scary to be honest nowadays. There's no clue what it may trigger for the person you are talking to at the time. However, it is very important to hear when someone has an unresolved crisis and you experience resistance from having an open conversation. It will appear like this:

- Their upbringing from family may have been very religious or traditional.

- They may not have any out LGBT people in their family and/or don't know any LGBT people personally.

- They may work in a very strict environment and feel no need for this conversation in the workplace.

- **Unresolved emotional feelings – personal roadblocks because LGBT people feel scary or different.**

It's hard to believe that someone would be scared of LGBT people! Nevertheless, it happens. It's good to have knowledge that it could occur with people surrounding you. The important thing to realize when you first openly discuss your views is to listen to the first couple of responses you get from someone. Ask about their knowledge or experience and LISTEN. People tell you who they are. It will appear like this:

- They don't know how to handle this perspective or quickly say they don't want to discuss it.

- They change the subject 100%.

- They tell you it's a lost cause for you to discuss it with them. No emotions are shown when they say it. You have hit a wall. It's called FEAR.

- **Perceived Threat- There could be an unwarranted feeling that you may act inappropriately and it makes them uncomfortable.**

As I said before, sexuality is a very hard topic in itself. Opening conversation about sexuality and gender identity will bring up a person's comfort about themselves. It's all in how you approach things. The best part to note is whether you have made someone feel any of the three things I have stated. Listening to body language, voice, and response is essential. If you perceive that they are threatened in any way, you now know you have hit one of the conflicts I have mentioned. It will appear like this:

- They may have faced an unwarranted advance in their past from a same sex individual.

- Take note of the surroundings – are many people around you or are you all alone?

- You may need to ask if the place you're having this conversation is comfortable or private enough.

---

### List the roadblock(s) you are or will be facing

_____

_____

_____

_____

_____

# CHAPTER 2
## Strategies for Having a Hard Conversation

1. **Be Prepared –Memorize 2 pointers**

   I can't say how much this comes into play!  Knowing your role and starting out on a strong foot are essential to the conversation.  If you support LGBT people getting their rights or you are an LGBT person talking about your rights, you have to know at least two main sentences that explain what you support.  Form your key messages about what you want this person to know.  Have them memorized.   Identify how you want to share your non-verbal and verbal communication.  Your energy will be used mostly on listening for their response and staying alert so you are ready with the next response.

2. **Keep your goals realistic**

   My motto is to keep it simple so you can keep up with the conversation.  If your goal is to talk to your father about supporting your gay brother marrying his partner and you know your father won't allow the gay son to bring his partner for dinner, change your goal.  Your goal should be to get your father to invite the son's partner to dinner.  The marriage conversation is for later!  Make your steps simple.

3. **Make a positive impression**

   Think about how you want this dialogue to come across as fair and firm.  It makes a difference. You want your dialogue to impress a person so they give some thought to what you said.  You want them to call you later or be open to more dialogue.  It helps when you have listened to them and given your point of view without dismissing their view.   They will entertain talking to you even when they have taken a stance opposite of yours.  Who knows, they may "evolve" one day.

4. **What to say, what to say!  Basic rules going in-**

As you prepare to invite someone into a conversation with you about support for LGBT people or to understand you better, the following pointers are necessary:

- Know some good facts or things they are interested in to get a general conversation happening.

- State why you wanted to have this conversation (remember your memorized messages).

- Look them in the eyes and LISTEN to their first response.

- Identify whether you heard any unresolved conflicts in that response.  Watch for non-verbal response.

- Then speak.

***Pointers for what to say in a personal roadblock scenario - roadblocks based on home/work or religious background.***

Scene:  Your friend David just told an anti-gay joke and you were appalled and insulted.  You had no idea a personal friend of yours didn't like "the gays"!  You want to talk to David about the anti-gay joke he made at dinner with 4 other friends where they called gay men "faggots."

**You:** ask David if you can talk with him alone.  Always ask for clarity about a situation first – "At lunch today, I thought I heard a joke you told about gay men and calling them "faggots."  Did you call gay men "faggots"?  LISTEN to their first response.

**DAVID:**  Yeah, I did, it was funny!   I can't stand gay people.

**YOU:**  I didn't find it funny.  I have been called names before and know we all have at some point in our lives.  Your jokes are usually very funny, but I didn't like you telling that type of joke.

**DAVID:**  It was just a joke, man.  No harm was done.  You aren't gay.

**YOU:**  That could have been my sister or brother you were talking about today.  I wouldn't want anyone saying anything negative about them.  I know you can understand.

**DAVID:**  Yes, I can.

**YOU:**  You are funny and we are friends, but can you cool down on the gay jokes?

**DAVID:** Maybe

**YOU:** I would appreciate it. Can you cool down on the gay jokes? PAUSE!!

**DAVID:** Ok.

The discussion above pointed out necessary pieces to address a personal roadblock. Clarity about the situation was done first, followed by hearing the response. If your goal is to address a verbal response, you have to be prepared with facts. One statement is all that was needed for David. Make sure you give time for a response. A pause gave David time to think and answer.

> *Pointers for what to say in an emotional roadblock scenario – roadblock based on LGBT people being perceived as scary or different.*

Scene: Your co-worker Leslie has confided to you that she doesn't like the transgender person working at the office. She's noticed "Michelle" in the women's restroom lately and is planning to report it to Human Resources because that's SCARY! She likes to see transgender people perform songs at the club, but not working and using the same space that she occupies during work hours. She doesn't want to discuss it because it feels "icky". You want to talk to her about why transgender people make her feel "icky". Your goal is to save Michelle's job. Ask what Leslie knows about the transgender community. LISTEN.

**YOU:** Leslie, I'm worried that you feel so terrified about our co-worker, Michelle.

**LESLIE:** Yeah, it has been on my mind. I don't understand why she can't go to the men's restroom since he is not a "real" woman. It feels creepy to me.

**YOU:** Why is it creepy when you know Michelle has been with the company for over one year. She is a real woman now.

**LESLIE:** I don't like to talk about it. It is just creepy.

**YOU:** I understand you may feel weird. Are you aware there are some books that share personal knowledge about what transgender people experience? I understand it is difficult to understand. They are going through a difficult time too.

**LESLIE:** I don't care. I have an appointment with Human Resources tomorrow.

**YOU:** You mean you don't understand? Can you delay the appointment?

**LESLIE:** Silence.

**YOU:** Can you at least agree to read a pamphlet about transgender people before going to Human Resources?  PAUSE!

**LESLIE:** I guess.

**YOU:** Ok.  I hear that you are frustrated.  I want to make sure you have education materials first.  It helped me a lot because I didn't understand either, but it is hard to walk around feeling you were born the wrong gender.

**LESLIE:** Alright, I will read your information.

**YOU:** Good, because she's a good worker and deserves her job and benefits just like we do.  We have to give her a chance.

*Pointers for what to say in a perceived threat scenario  - roadblocks based on unwarranted feelings that you may act inappropriately.*

Scene:  You have just told your best friend, Jamie that you are a lesbian.  Both of you are college roommates.  The two of you have shared everything from drinks at the bar to the bathroom.  Now, she won't stay in the room alone with you.   Some friends have informed you that she thinks you may have a crush on her.  You want to make sure she knows you are her best friend.  Being a lesbian does not mean that you are attracted to every woman you meet.  START THE CONVERSATION in a public setting.

**YOU:** Jamie, let's get something to eat, I'm hungry.

**JAMIE:** Ok.

**YOU:** I noticed you haven't been yourself the past month.  I hope things are ok?  PAUSE.

**JAMIE:** Yes.  I am fine.  I thought you have been acting funny lately.

**YOU:** Me?  Well, I did want to talk again since I told you that I was a lesbian.  I didn't want you to be scared of me!

**JAMIE:** Oh, I'm not scared.  We are good.  I have just been busy, so what's on your mind?

**YOU:** Good.  I am so glad we have each other's back!  I'm so grateful for our friendship.  I want you to know, I will never do anything to break up our friendship.  I have heard that some people think I may be attracted to you.  I am hoping you know just because I am a lesbian does not mean that I am attracted to every woman I know.  PAUSE! GIVE HER TIME TO RESPOND.  LISTEN.

**JAMIE:** Well, what if you are in some way?

**YOU:** We are the best of friends. That's us. You are like my sister.

**JAMIE:** I was wondering.

**YOU:** Don't wonder. I am your friend.

Having a difficult conversation doesn't mean you have to have a lot of words to say. It means you must be clear on your goal. If your goal is to make sure a friend feels safe alone with you because you are a lesbian, deliver on that goal. Create safe spaces in a room alone. Don't crowd her space. Don't let her attempt to crowd your space. Ask questions when things happen out of the ordinary.

---

**List your top 3 strategies for having a hard conversation:**

_____

_____

_____

_____

_____

---

# CHAPTER 3
## The Art of Arguing

Dialogue is precious. I believe it is one of the most intimate ways to understand a person. If done correctly, you can feel the exchange of mental thought and revel in presenting difference without losing your dignity. You can survive arguments in a healthy way. It is a matter of feeling confident about and ready for difficult conversations. This is the point of no return. What you say will stick in a person's mind. After having an intense conversation, there will be two things a person always remembers:

1. What you said and 2) how they were treated.

Let's face it, fighting for your rights has never been easy. It's this tug of war on viewpoints that makes it hard to stay in the moment while in the conversation. The sweetness is that it can change the scope of a situation. Getting to that scope of change is intense. This is the place that I used to break down and cry. Yep, I said it! One time, a lot of people supported me in meeting with an opponent of marriage equality in the civil rights community. He was one of the men around Rev. Dr. Martin Luther King during the 1960s. I had fought hard to get in the room with him because I heard he was not supportive of our issue.

I got my chance. He met with me a few minutes before preparing for the annual August celebration of the March on Washington. I didn't have practice or know the art of arguing tips, I just had CHUTZPAH. Well, it takes more. It takes knowing the art of discussion. I fumbled through identifying my key concerns by saying long run-on sentences. He couldn't figure out the points I was trying to make. I added other topics into the conversation, which didn't make sense in sticking with my theme. My voice volume became low because I lost confidence in myself. He had to ask me to repeat myself two times.

I broke down crying after I left the room. It was not my best moment. However, I learned a great lesson – preparation and practice help you build confidence. Knowing tips on how to have a difficult conversation can change things. It is great to have passion, but knowing how to have the dialogue is essential. Simply put- know the art of arguing.

Here are the tips you need to know and remember when you begin to talk. If you keep at least four tips in your head, you will do a great job.

*TIPS for the Art of Arguing:*

- Hear what they said, repeat it back to them if necessary for clarity.

- Identify their key concerns with no accusations.

- Don't forget to breathe.

- Make your point in 1-2 sentences and stick with that theme.

- Let them finish expressing their concerns.

- Use affirming language when their point is completed, then offer another view point.

- Offer solutions or personal stories that support your points.

- Don't forget to breathe.

- Do NOT lose your cool!!! Maintain calmness. You will outwardly appear confident and that shows power and respect.

- Ask for explanations of their views and don't be afraid to offer your solutions in order to bridge some solid ground between the different views.

- Remain positive and calm even if there is no agreement.

- Be cordial even if you're disappointed and it is ok to say you are disappointed. Also say you appreciated the person's willingness to discuss the issue.

- Don't forget to shake hands or say "thank you for talking."

- Look people in their eyes when you end the discussion. It conveys respect.

## KNOW WHEN TO PAUSE!

Another important piece to having a difficult discussion is knowing when to listen or stop. I have learned from my experience that sometimes saying less means more. If you have made a point and you know it – be quiet! Maybe they are digesting your point or they are baffled. You don't know and you shouldn't assume you know. LISTEN. This is where the PAUSE comes into play. Whenever you make a substantial point, PAUSE.

After you have made a substantial point, pause for 6 seconds to listen for their feedback.

Look a person in the eye when you pause so you connect with them.

It is ok for a little quietness or uncomfortable pause to occur. Sometimes, mind change happens during pauses.

Let them speak first. Not you. You want a response.

## Example-

I had a conversation with Sharon, a union member who didn't support gays getting married. The union member had a son who was gay and I knew she was supportive of her son having a boyfriend. I asked how is it you are supportive of your son, but you don't want him to have legal rights with his boyfriend?

**SHARON:** I believe in the Bible and my church. My Bible didn't support gays getting married.

**ME:** I pointed out the state's religious exemption that articulates no church will be forced to marry a gay couple. The civil marriage will be conducted by a civil court. No religious ceremony has to happen. Therefore, her son's rights could be protected.

**SHARON:** I still don't support gays getting married.

ME: You can still support your belief and your son's life at the same time. I'm sure he would never want your church to marry him. They have a right to say no. Your son though- he has a right to a good life with all civil rights- just the way you thought when you birthed him into the world.

**SHARON:** Hmmmm….

PAUSE! Sharon was given something to think about and was on the brink of changing her mind. It may not come now. It may come later. But I was confident. I had made a point.

**SHARON:** Well, I will think about this. I don't know what to say. I do want my son to have a good life.

**ME:** I appreciate us talking about this! I'm glad you will think about this. It takes time and conversations like ours to evolve on this. Let's connect next week?

**SHARON:** Yes, I do want to talk again. I may be able to do this now.

End dialogue. Follow up.

## TIME

It is always good to keep a discussion less than one hour. If you can't end a difficult conversation in one hour, you are approaching unsafe territory. Everyone's energy wears down after one hour and sensitivities heighten. Tempers flare and miscommunications occur quickly when you have gone past an hour of discussion. The ideal time would be 45 minutes and then take a 15 minute break or agree to have discussions anywhere from a day later to one week later. My best responses have always followed after a 45 minute conversation at most. It gives you enough time to present your thoughts and fully hear someone's views so they don't feel slighted.

## TONE

I have always found it useful to be aware of your tone when discussing LGBT issues. If you are beginning the hard conversation with a friend or family member and your voice volume drops, it conveys fear or that you are scared! Just RELAX. You are embarking on one conversation that will turn out positive because you will spark many other conversations with friends or family on the topic. This is why it's important to work on your tone.

Here's what I have found helpful. Take note of how you always sound to family or friends when enjoying a good day spending quality time together. Maybe recall a time you all played a game of cards or went on a camping trip together or enjoyed fun at a family outing. Keep the tone of your voice in mind and practice keeping near this tone during difficult conversations. Be aware when your tone changes. Take a deep breathe to bring the tone back to an even pitch so you convey you are open for more discussion and not show you are defensive. I know this is hard. The more times you have LGBT discussions, the easier this will get.

# CHAPTER 4
## Rehearsal Time

Preparation teaches you to be confident. You now have all the tools you need to have a difficult conversation. The opportunities will present themselves easily and you can now feel at ease in approaching the topic. Let's practice! Here are a set of scripts to get you started. You will see some blank spaces so you can write your own scripts for your specific situations. I strongly urge you to do this since it helps to form your own experiences.

### *SCENE 1*

**YOU:** Preparing to have a conversation with your friend Joshua, that doesn't know you are an LGBT ally. You aren't sure whether he is supportive of the issue or not. The first thing to do is to start the conversation.

**YOU-** Hey Joshua, did you know that I recently got involved with the No-Hate campaign in our state?

**JOSHUA-** No, I didn't. What is it?

**YOU-** It is to support the LGBT community from being discriminated against. I have been active in fighting inequality against the LGBT community every since I learned that my husband and I receive over 1,000 rights and benefits of marriage and they can't. It's really hard on a relationship when there's no equality for it.

**JOSHUA-** Well, are you gay or something? I mean, what are you doing? Don't you have some other causes you could fight?

**YOU–** Of course there are other causes I support. I also support the LGBT community and let me tell you what's happening now…….

**WRITE YOUR OWN DIALOGUE:**

_____

_____

_____

_____

_____

_____

_____

_____

_____

## *SCENE 2*

**YOU (male):**  Preparing to have a conversation with your brother, Jeffrey about you being Bisexual. It has taken some time for you to feel comfortable about telling your family who you are.  Now, you are ready to talk to your brother.  You are ready to live openly, so you call your brother.

**YOU:**  Jeffrey, I know I have been a little distant lately.  I wanted to tell you what's been going on in my life.

**Jeffrey:**  Sure.  I was wondering what was up.

**YOU:**  You know I had dated Jessica a couple of years ago.   I've had a lot of changes happening for me recently.  It's not like us to not talk.  I always want to keep the communication good between us.   I'm dating again now and I feel really good about it.  I'm dating a man right now.

**Jeffrey:**  WHAT!  You never mentioned anything about liking men.  What's going on with you?

**YOU:** Nothing but good is happening for me, Jeffrey. I realized that I had an attraction to men too. I'm not trying to confuse anyone. I like both sexes, so I want to be honest with you. Nothing has changed about the person you know. You know me!

**Jeffrey:** This is a lot to take in. When did this happen? Do mom and dad know?

**YOU:** I know it's a lot to take in right now. I would like to have the opportunity to talk with mom and dad soon. Please let me talk to them directly before you call. I love you all and want you all in my life. Here's how you can support me as I talk to everyone. Give him a plan of how you want his support.

PAUSE. Listen.

**WRITE YOUR OWN DIALOGUE:**

_____

_____

_____

_____

_____

_____

_____

_____

## SCENE 3

**YOU:** Having a conversation with your Pastor about his sermon last Sunday. He said that LGBT people were "prostitutes" and fell short of God's glory. You have been in this church for 2 years and you want him to accept you as a child of God.

**YOU:** Thank you so much for meeting with me Rev. Gotpraise. Thank you so much for your leadership. I really love our church. As you know, I haven't missed many Sundays here because I am enjoying receiving the word from your preaching. I want to make sure you know this upfront.

**Rev. Gotpraise:** Thank you so much Rita! Our church has grown a lot and I appreciate your commitment.

**YOU:** I asked to meet with you because of your sermon last Sunday. You were speaking from the Bible- Galatians, and stated that there were different kinds of sins. You listed LGBT people being the same as prostitutes and said we all fell short of God's glory. I had never heard that from you before and was surprised that you would attack the LGBT community in this way. Why did you say such harsh words?

**Rev. Gotpraise:** I wasn't attacking LGBT people. I didn't intend to be harsh. I was telling God's truth that LGBT people have sinned and it falls in the category with prostitutes. Prostitutes can be redeemed! There is a path for all to change their ways and receive God's love.

**YOU:** Rev. Gotpraise, I am a lesbian and I don't view myself as a prostitute. I know there are other LGBT people in our congregation. Our church must be a safe place for everyone. But I didn't feel safe after that sermon. Are you saying that all LGBT are not accepted into this church as loving whole people like everyone else?

**Rev. Gotpraise:** I am saying that you are welcome. However, according to the Bible, you are a sinner and would have to change your ways to receive God's love. I don't want you to leave us. You belong with us, we will just have to work towards your lifestyle changing to receive all of God's love.

**YOU:** I am a child of God already. I don't need to be changed. I guess you are saying that I can continue to pay tithes here while you continue to not hear that I am God's child no matter my sexual orientation or gender identity. Is that true?

**Rev. Gotpraise:** We need you and your tithes at the church. There is room here for everyone. What is it that I can say to make you feel comfortable?

**YOU:** Sermons that state I am a sinner or that I am equivalent to a "prostitute" or not welcome to receive God's love is not acceptable. It sends a hurtful message to the LGBT community. I would like to share with you sermons from other Ministers that have Affirming Churches. Are you open to hearing about Affirming Communities of Faith?

**Rev. Gotpraise:** I still have some doubts Rita, but I am open to hearing how I can make LGBT people feel comfortable in our church. No one has ever spoken to me about my sermons to the LGBT community. I don't want to be called a homophobe! Let me see their sermons.

**YOU:** I am glad we had this conversation. There are ways to make the LGBT community feel welcome in our church. Can we work towards this goal together? I would like to meet with you again in 2 weeks to discuss what you have read about Affirming Communities of Faith and what they say to LGBT people. Maybe I can introduce you to some Affirming Pastors?

**Rev. Gotpraise:** Let me read this first and let's talk in 2 weeks. You have given me a lot of things to think about. I promise to review the papers and meet with you again.

**YOU:** Ok. We can meet in 2 weeks. I look forward to our next discussion. Thank you for listening to me about how to make LGBT people feel safe in our church. See you next Sunday!

Follow up. You have just had a difficult conversation that may lead to change.


**WRITE YOUR OWN DIALOGUE:**

_____

_____

_____

_____

_____

_____

_____

_____

## SCENE 4

**YOU:**  Having a conversation with an elected politician official to ask for his support on an anti-discrimination law in your state.  You noticed that he hasn't made any public statements on the anti-discrimination law and you want to know where he stands.

**YOU:** Thank you so much for meeting with me Representative Japuki.  I noticed you go to my sister's church.  She's been a member for 2 years.

**ELECTED OFFICIAL:**  Yes, I do attend that church! My family has been going for 10 years.

**YOU:** My sister said she saw your wife there 2 weeks ago.  My sister and I support this anti-discrimination law that is inclusive of LGBT rights.   I see that you have not signed on to support the bill.

**ELECTED OFFICIAL:**  No, I haven't signed because of my religious beliefs.  I'm not sure many would support in our state.

**YOU:**  Well, as I just stated, my sister is religious and she supports the bill.  The bill has a religious exemption clause.  I'm sure you know about this, right?

**ELECTED OFFICIAL:**  Yes, but I am still skeptical.  I don't know if it's enough.  I am thinking about it.

**YOU:**  I would like to help clear up any doubts.  Can we discuss your hesitancy on the bill?  I know a lot of my religious family and friends have supported me in my journey.   Can I set up a meeting with you and some of my supportive religious family and friends?    Here is a packet of talking points in support of the bill.

**ELECTED OFFICIAL:**  I am open to hearing more.  Yes, please do.  I need to hear more voices on this.


**WRITE YOUR OWN DIALOGUE:**

_____

_____

_____

## SCENE 5

You want to tell your Mom that you have a girlfriend now and you want to bring her to the family reunion.

**YOU:** Mom, I know you have met my girlfriend. Do you like her?

**MOM:** Yes, she's nice.

**YOU:** Well, I like her a lot and things are working out great with us. I wanted to invite her to our family reunion. I've been dating her for 6 months now and feel good about asking her to join me there.

**MOM:** Are you crazy? Our family isn't ready for that foolishness. Can you just keep that secret with us right now. I don't know if your Aunt Josie is ready for this.

**YOU:** Mom, you know I love you right? I think our family gets ready for this by actually going through getting to know us together.

**MOM:** I disagree. They aren't ready. Don't you bring that girl to our family reunion.

**YOU:** Mom, I hear you. What is it that bothers you about my girlfriend attending the family reunion?

**MOM:** They just don't accept anything that is not of the traditional family. I don't want you ridiculed at the family reunion.

**YOU:** I feel really strongly about being ready to be who I am with the entire family. I don't want to be ashamed of being who I am. Maybe we can talk to Aunt Josie before the reunion. That would be helpful in getting her prepared for this change because I'm part of the family values too!

**MOM:** Hmmm…Ok, I will go along with this. We will call Aunt Josie next week.

Let mom rest and think! You have gotten her through a changing moment.

**WRITE YOUR OWN DIALOGUE:**

_____

_____

_____

_____

_____

_____

_____

_____

## *SCENE 6*

This is a big one! I will incorporate having 2 difficult conversations to improve understanding.

A co-worker, Stan next to your cubicle told you that he wasn't going to eat with Malik anymore because he saw pictures of Malik and his boyfriend on the desk. It was too public! This was inappropriate for the office- according to Stan. Stan was also calling the Human Resources dept about this matter and asked you not to say anything to Malik. You have to respond to Stan and Malik. Your goal is to support Malik in being open in the workplace. You also want Stan to become aware of inclusive workplace policies. This is Malik's life and job. He deserves to feel comfortable in the workplace.

**YOU:** Stan, are you serious that you don't want to have lunch with Malik because of this?

**STAN:** Yes. I am for everyone's rights, but not in my face so blatantly. He can do this in private.

**YOU:** What exactly bothers you about him sharing his life in pictures on his desk?

**STAN:** I can't take it being public. If feels like he is pushing his lifestyle down my throat.

**YOU:** Well, I understand being shocked. However, you have your wife and kid's photo on your desk. What are you going to say when all of us have family pictures on our desks?

**STAN:** I know, but our pictures are normal. His is different.

**YOU:** It is different, but he's normal too. AND, this isn't a "lifestyle" for him, this is his life. Being gay is not a "lifestyle". PAUSE!

**STAN:** Ugh! What are we going to do when he wants to bring his "friend" to the Holiday Party?

**YOU:** I am hoping you consider including him in every activity of our company. I will. This is his family and I don't want to harm anyone's family. Do you?

**STAN:** I had not considered this his family.

**YOU:** His family is in the picture on his desk to remind him of home, just like you have your family picture on your desk reminding you of home. Perhaps we can talk to Malik over lunch and hear about his life and family before you turn him over to Human Resources? Would you do this with me?

**STAN:** I will do it with you, but I don't like him being public.

**YOU:** It would be less threatening to find out more about him and his life before YOU go to Human Resources. I am not supporting you going to Human Resources, but I do support you in learning more about Malik first. I like him.

**STAN:** I don't understand how you like him so much.

**YOU:** He's a good guy and is our co-worker. He has helped our company a lot too. I don't understand why you feel threatened by a picture. Why does this bother you?

**STAN:** I had a friend that was gay once and then he made a pass at me!

**YOU:** You think Malik will just make a pass at you? You have placed everyone in your friend's shoes?

**STAN:** Well….

**YOU:** He's not your friend that made a pass at you. He is a gay man with his boyfriend's picture on his desk. He is not here to threaten us. Can you give him the opportunity to be honest and open at work? Will you trust me to set up lunch and listen to him?

**STAN:** Ok, set up lunch.

**TALK WITH MALIK IN PRIVATE**

**YOU:** Malik, Stan and I noticed the picture of you and your "friend" on your desk. Have you gotten any responses or funny looks from some of our co-workers?

**MALIK:** Yes, I have! Some people are not talking to me anymore. I have been cut from the co-worker "social outings" list too. I didn't know there were so many homophobic people in this building. Our company policy is inclusive, but I guess that is in writing only.

**YOU:** I'm sorry Malik. I would like to be helpful. I am your friend and will support you through this. I am an ally.

**MALIK:** Thank you for saying this. At least I know who I can trust.

**YOU:** To be honest, Stan had some issues with your picture also. We have talked about it and he wants to hear what is happening for you over lunch. Are you willing to have lunch with both of us?

**MALIK:** Yes.

**TALK BACK TO STAN-----------**

**YOU:** Stan, I have talked to Malik and he has experienced our co-workers not speaking to him anymore. I think this is a good time for you to hear how it feels to be excluded before you go to Human Resources.

**STAN:** I had no idea others were treating him this way. I want to hear what he is going through.

**YOU:** Ok. I am asking you to listen before you pass judgment on him. I am also asking for you to be understanding because this is his life and his job. The Human Resources Policy is inclusive of sexual orientation.  This is something we all can work towards acceptance on together.  Are you ready for lunch?

**STAN:**  Yes.  I won't say anything crazy.

**YOU:**  Great.  I will set up lunch for the end of the week.

How would you handle a complicated dialogue among 1-3 people?  Handle it one step at a time.  Identify the fear they feel.  Identify your goal for the conversation.   Have the conversations.

**WRITE YOUR OWN DIALOGUE:**

_____

_____

_____

_____

_____

_____

_____

# CHAPTER 5
## What Not To Say!

It's come to the moment that you are ready to go speak up about yourself or about the LGBT cause. It's understandable that you may fill some jitters. Before you move forward, I have some short advice on what NOT to say. There will be times that you experience frustration, setbacks in the conversation, and disappointment from family members, co-workers, companies, or close friends. It is expected on this journey. So, be mindful of some things not to say. Some words or actions will break down any bridge you try to build towards a positive outcome.

***Here's my list of things NOT TO SAY or do:***

- This is discrimination and you are wrong!

- I hate this place and job! You don't treat people right here.

- Talk to the Hand. I don't want to hear your explanation to discriminate.

- Get out of my face with that Bible stuff.

- I hate you!

- Have a temper tantrum.

- Scream or shout profanity.

# CHAPTER 6
## You Are Ready

It's all about your delivery now! It would good for you to practice with a friend by doing a role play of the discussion. Make sure you write out your dialogue before so you are ready to role play with a friend. Have your pointers and identify your positions. Be aware of your body language and keep your tone open during the discussion. Confidence will show and respect will be mutual. You are on the right side of history and I'm with you in spirit too!

### CLOSING

At the start of this guide it may have been hard to see yourself getting through a difficult discussion without panicking. Trust me, I have been there, done that, and bought the t-shirt! You don't have to worry anymore about whether you will be able to say what needs to be said. You have now completed learning all the ins and outs.

The guide has taught you to first identify whether the person you are talking to has unresolved or perceived emotional baggage. I have covered three major organizing skills in preparing for your intent in the conversation and reaching your goal. You have lots of scripts to help you form responses to a variety of situations. All of this will build your confidence while having difficult conversations about LGBT discrimination.

With practice and this guide, you can handle family, friends, co-workers, and religious and political leaders. There will be many opportunities for you to have conversations about supporting the LGBT community. At this time in history, more healthy dialogue is needed so everyone understands that LGBT discrimination is not acceptable. Remember, it only takes a few minutes of conversation to change hearts and minds. You can now do this with confidence.

GOOD LUCK!

# BIOGRAPHY
## – Donna R. Payne

As one of the Human Rights Campaign's key representatives, Payne works closely with Civil Rights organizations and leaders and with a number of organizations across the country to increase visibility of the lesbian, gay, bisexual and transgender community within the religious and people of color communities. She has lead HRC's work on HRC's Historically Black Colleges and Universities Program in supporting LGBT students on their campus and addressing concerns with HBCU administrators. Donna is a noted speaker in the LGBT community and has written articles nationwide on being an LGBT Civil Rights African American lesbian. She is a founding board member of the National Black Justice Coalition - a civil rights organization dedicated to empowering Black lesbian, gay, bisexual, and transgender people.

Donna has received many awards for her transformational organizing work without regard for race, sexual orientation, gender identity or age. In 2009, she received the Capitol Pride Hero award in Washington, DC and was nominated by The Root.com as one of 100 established black Americans who are making exceptional contributions in their professions and communities. In 2011, she received the Rosa Parks Award for her coalition building skills with Civil Rights groups and Historically Black Colleges and Universities (HBCU's). In 2012, she received the National Action Network's Woman of Excellence Award from Rev. Al Sharpton and was named one of the Top Twenty Black LGBT Movers and Shakers.

Payne is an activist who is originally from Memphis, TN. She graduated from the University of Tennessee, Knoxville in 1986 with a degree in Political Science. She has served the political community by working with the Young Democrats in Washington, DC, the Political Congress of Black Women and on Congressional campaigns in the south. She volunteered with the Clinton administration during its national health care reform efforts at the White House. Ms Payne is also a member of the Metropolitan Community Church of Washington, DC and resides in Maryland.

To order additional copies of this book, contact:
Xlibris Corporation
1-888-795-4274
www.Xlibris.com
Orders@Xlibris.com